1
My background

For the first nine years of my teaching career my background in mathematics learning—the way maths was taught to me—was the sole foundation on which I built the teaching of maths to the children in my care.

Mathematics had always been the subject of the chosen few, and I wasn't one of them. I managed to survive through my high school years with as little maths as possible and, in some areas, with little or no understanding. When I entered teachers college, I specialised in the education of children aged from two to eight years. I remember thinking at the time, 'How much maths could they possibly need?' When I entered the work force I was pleased, and even relieved, to find teachers' manuals, blackline masters and, when all else failed, the *Woolies teach your children maths* books 1, 2 and 3.

As I began to observe and listen to children and my peers, I realised that while we expect all children to walk, talk, read and write, we don't expect them all to be mathematically inclined. Enough maths to get by in everyday life is often deemed adequate.

As my teaching career progressed, I began to make judgments about preferred teaching styles. My confidence in what I was doing increased and I began to voice these opinions in the staffroom.

Further study seemed the natural progression and I chose the area of language. In my first year of teaching I had been confronted with a very stilted, unrealistic way of teaching children to read—words in colour. Deep down I knew there had to be a more natural way and so I sought to find it, study it and implement it. The result was a classroom alive with language. All of Cambourne's 'conditions for learning' were in force. The children became active participants, in charge of their own learning. I had high expectations of them where language was concerned and they performed accordingly.

In the course of each day there was a time for mathematics. This was a time that was distinctly different from the rest of the active, discussing, reacting, experimenting, child-centred environment of the language classroom. Mathematics was teacher-centred and teacher-directed, a time when children listened, copied and worked in relative silence. I didn't enjoy it; they couldn't possibly have enjoyed it. I managed to cover the curriculum requirements in a very basic, straightforward way

'Oh no, maths!'

DEVELOPING CONFIDENCE IN MATHEMATICS

Francesca Murphy

ASHTON SCHOLASTIC
SYDNEY AUCKLAND NEW YORK TORONTO LONDON

The author wishes to thank the children, parents and teachers from the following schools in New South Wales for the recordings and letters contained in this text: Our Lady of the Rosary, Fairfield; Sacred Heart, Cabramatta; and Mary Immaculate, Bossley Park.

Murphy, Francesca
'Oh no, maths!' Developing confidence in mathematics.

ISBN 0 86896 808 0

1. Mathematics—study and teaching (primary).
I. Title. (Series: M3 mathematics: mapping mathematical meaning.)

372.7044

First published in 1991 by Ashton Scholastic Pty Limited A.C.N. 000 614 577, PO Box 579, Gosford 2250. Also in Brisbane, Melbourne, Adelaide, Perth and Auckland, NZ.

Cover photograph by Ken Dolling.
Printed by Brown Prior Anderson Pty Ltd, Burwood, Victoria.
Typeset in Goudy.
12 11 10 9 8 7 6 5 4 3 2 1   1 2 3 4 5 / 9

Contents

Figure 1.1

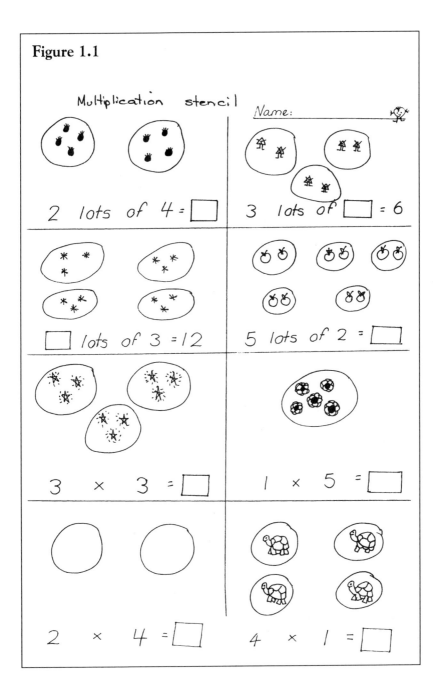

Multiplication stencil

Name: _____

2 lots of 4 = ☐

3 lots of ☐ = 6

☐ lots of 3 = 12

5 lots of 2 = ☐

3 × 3 = ☐

1 × 5 = ☐

2 × 4 = ☐

4 × 1 = ☐

and, when in doubt, I referred back to memories of the way I had been taught. I relied heavily on worksheets. I knew children had to be able to visualise numbers and see them in a realistic way. My idea of realism was the worksheet (see Figure 1.1).

1 The children were given a multiplication stencil.
2 If they couldn't grasp the concept through the stencil, they used pencils, crayons or whatever else was lying around to illustrate the concept.
3 Once I believed the children had a basic understanding, then 'practice makes perfect'.

Looking back now, I see the faults in my teaching of maths. Because of my insecurities I needed order and structure and I relied on my basic ability to teach what was in the curriculum. I looked at what the children produced to evaluate my teaching rather than their learning and didn't consider the way their thinking was developing. For example, if a child was working with dice, rolling one of them twice and adding the score of each throw, they might record this in the following way—4, 3, 7. I would have to introduce the + sign, as otherwise it would make no sense to me. Now, however, I would recognise the child's ability to add 4 and 3 and to represent it in a meaningful way.

I remember the negative feelings about maths which I brought to every lesson. I resented stopping a productive language lesson to do maths. I also remember getting results—of a different standard to the results I get now, but results nonetheless.

For example,
from this:

4 + 3 = 7
9 + 2 = 11
4 + 1 = 5
17 + 2 = 19
7 – 3 = 4
11 – 2 = 9
5 – 1 = 4
19 – 2 = 17

which showed children's ability in arithmetic, to the example as shown in Figure 1.2. This illustrates a child's understanding of the Base Ten system and the need to 'bundle' numbers into groups of ten in

Figure 1.2

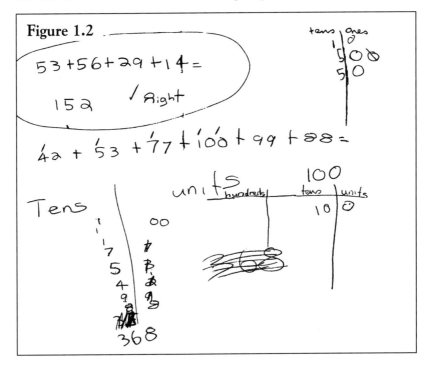

order to make addition easier, even though 42 + 53 + 77 + 100 + 99 + 88 does not equal 368.

My children always met the requirements for the grade. What more could have been expected? I felt there had to be a better approach. I wanted the entire teaching day to be child-centred, with the children taking responsibility for their own learning. I had successfully done this with language lessons. I believed similar results could be achieved with maths.

I recall the day (at the end of 1986) when my principal called me into her office for our yearly assessment, where we would review individual personal strengths and weaknesses. Mathematics once again became a topic of concern.

The year 1987 marked the most significant change in my teaching life, my professional life and, to an extent, my personal life. It was in this year that the Catholic Education Office (Sydney) conducted its numeracy project. My school was asked to nominate a teacher to become a member of the team of 27 teachers and, because of my 'interest', I was invited to become involved.

My initial reaction was one of almost terror. 'Oh no, maths!' As I heard about the 25 release days involved over the course of the year, my interest grew. I didn't think mathematics upgrading could be all that involved. It perhaps required a look at new materials on the market; a few mentals books or new blackline masters. After all, I thought, maths is straightforward. I was soon to learn differently!

My principal and I attended the two introductory days of the numeracy project. We learnt how the various regional consultants reviewed different programs on the market; and discussed the philosophy and ideas of Helen Pengelly, from South Australia. She is regarded as being the most 'in line' with the current thinking of Sydney's Catholic Education Office. Her philosophy outlines an approach to learning mathematics which comes from a child's point of view, and so places the emphasis on the personal experiences each child has with mathematics.

Helen stood up and, after a few brief words, gave us a maths task to perform. I went into a panic. I was about to display my inadequacies in front of not only my peers, but my principal.

Looking back now, the task was simple enough: break into groups of five, choose something each of you has in common and record it in three different ways.

Simple enough? In retrospect it seems so, but at that time it gave me the greatest feeling of insecurity I had ever experienced. I hadn't come to actually do any maths. I had come to learn about the best way to teach it. I didn't need to know it to be able to demonstrate it.

I somehow managed to disguise my panic and busied myself with the task of organising the information my group members had supplied, not knowing where or how they had derived it.

Helen pointed out that from the large group of people at the conference there were some who would have drawn information from a vast background of formal mathematics, some who would have drawn from a vast background of infants mathematics, and some who would have found it difficult to draw from much at all. We would, however, be working together to gain some insight into children's mathematical thinking. I only wanted to make a quick getaway.

'Official teaching hierarchy have the tendency to be away from the real life of the classroom for too long,' I said to my principal. 'They have too much time to investigate the possibilities of perfection in that classroom and too much authority to impose it on others. In other words, she doesn't know what it's all about. I'm getting out of here.'

My principal smiled. I was there to stay.

During those two days I came to realise that I was expected to change in ways I didn't think possible in the area of mathematics. This was the philosophy put forward by the numeracy project:

◊ children are learners
◊ children learn mathematics at their own rate
◊ children learn through personal experience with mathematical ideas
◊ mathematical learning is developmental
◊ children approximate towards mathematical concepts
◊ interaction facilitates learning

◊ learners require feedback which values the learner
◊ children are responsible for their own learning
◊ the environment needs to support and challenge the learner
◊ attitudes affect learning.

Numeracy working project, February 1987

Although I believed in each of these points, my experience was limited to areas outside mathematics. It frightened me. I felt that I needed to be a mathematician before any of this could make sense.

It was also made clear that the emphasis would be on the learning rather than on the teaching of mathematics. I couldn't see the difference: to me, the two terms were interchangeable.

I decided that by keeping a low profile, and disguising my limited knowledge, I could go unnoticed. I would take on ideas that I found useful and 'dress up' old ideas. I would survive.

2
Starting to change

Following those first two panic-stricken days of initiation, I calmed down and began to look more closely at what I was doing in the classroom. I was using some concrete materials, but their use was directed. I wasn't allowing the children time to play with, experiment with and manipulate materials in the ways that they wanted. I was using an activity-based approach, following ideas from a text, with an emphasis on achieving the correct answer at all times.

After only two days of inservice, I decided to trial the idea of letting the children take control of their own learning.

I had heard a lot about patterning, so I decided to start small and allow my Year 2 class to pattern. I remember the task clearly.

'Make me a pattern of 9, repeated three times.

Use whatever materials you need.'

This was the open invitation these children had been waiting for; the opportunity to build, sort and even throw materials around. When I insisted on the results of the task being recorded, I opened Pandora's box.

'What's a pattern?'
'What do you mean?'
'How do you do it?'
'Is this right?'
'I don't understand.'

It was a complete disaster and served only to convince me more than ever that the chalk-and-talk method had great merit.

With the exception of a few cosmetic alterations, maths time in 2S continued much the same as it had before my experiment. There was more discussion from the children and more opportunities to record things in their own ways, but I still controlled the teaching.

Part two of the inservice course began. Each day started with maths tasks, and making coffee was often my only contribution. I thought that I must be the only teacher in Sydney who had managed to slip through an entire educational life with minimal maths. I felt like a fraud who had cheated her children out of mathematics. All the others were grasping what was going on, but it was all slipping past me.

I remember having dinner with a friend that

week. I was so unusually quiet that she asked what was wrong. Straight away I burst into tears. I simply couldn't cope.

The entire experience of mathematics and change, teaching and learning and processes and control, was too much. It was at this stage that I became aware of what children must go through when faced with the expectation to perform even when the directions are incomprehensible. What do we as teachers say to them? 'Ask and I'll help you.' I had to admit my lack of knowledge and ask for help, regardless of the reaction from my peers. I was no longer avoiding the issue and almost instantly my frustrations began to subside. Others were also experiencing fears and frustrations and I realised that I had been so busy trying to hide that I wasn't listening to what was going on around me.

I re-examined my own philosophy of teaching alongside that of the numeracy project and began to see the similarities. Then I closely examined my personal attitudes towards maths and decided that I would never pass those attitudes on to another child. It wouldn't be easy, but I had to change.

The value of support became very evident. Helen was there to encourage, discuss and de-mystify problems—but never to give answers or make decisions. It had taken me from March to July to become convinced that I needed to change. From then on I was to gain control of that change in very small steps.

I needed to examine what my children were

already doing, what they needed to know and how I could help them to achieve results in maths in a way in which I was comfortable.

3
Base Ten

It was Helen who suggested that Base Ten was an appropriate starting point because it would encompass a wide range of necessary number knowledge.

I decided to start with a small group and initially chose children who had already displayed the ability to communicate their thoughts clearly.

The children were asked to gather popsticks into bundles of ten. This seemed logical, because ten is the basis of our number system. This became the ideal situation in which to ask the children how many bundles they had and how many popsticks they had altogether. Some could count by ten; those who couldn't unbundled the sticks and counted each one. The children didn't seem intimidated by those around them, as they worked at their own pace.

When I felt the children were ready to proceed, the Base Ten board and two dice were introduced. The first rule was also established: no more than nine popsticks were allowed in the ones column. The children were quick to make the connection between this rule and the initial bundling they had done. Seeing that the children were progressing gave me the confidence to continue.

It was then time to introduce the second rule: no more than nine bundles of ten were allowed in the tens column. This is where my first real fear appeared. Would the children see the connection between ten and a hundred? After all, we had done no bundling of hundreds. Here is a conversation between Alfina, Natalie and the teacher about what to do with more than nine bundles of ten.

Alfina: If you got nine bundles of ten, if you get ten more, you've got a hundred.

Teacher: But you can't have those tens in that column (the tens column). What are you going to do with them?

Alfina: (pause) Ah... you put them back.

Natalie: I've got a good idea. I just tried it out. You get all your popstick bundles. You get another elastic band and you put it all over, because they fit inside the bundle.

Alfina: What's that 'unit' there for?

Teacher: Unit means one.

Alfina: Then you put it in ones.

Teacher: But you can't have more than nine bundles of ten.

Alfina: You put it under the unit because it's one.

Teacher: It's one big bundle, but how many have
        you got in there?
Alfina: A hundred.
Teacher: Where would you put the hundred? When
        you had too many ones, you made another
        column.
Alfina: But Miss Sergi, you do exactly the same.
Teacher: What is exactly the same?
Alfina: I don't know, but you do exactly the same.
Peter: (*who had been listening, intervened*) Ten
        and hundred.

This illustrates the understanding that was
taking place.

Throughout the initial work with Base Ten, it
became evident that the children needed the
chance to experiment at their own level. They also
needed time to talk with each other and to the
teacher. The opportunity to think out loud was a
very important element of their learning and
allowed the children to consolidate what they knew.
I had the chance to talk and listen to each child
individually while monitoring their results.

It was here that more concerns appeared. These
children needed to record the work they were doing.
Up until now they had recorded algorithmic
computations in their maths books—neatly ruled
and all uniform in method. This meant that the
school administration and parents could see exactly
what the children knew and could do. The
children's recordings now looked like those in
Figures 3.1–3.6.

Figure 3.1

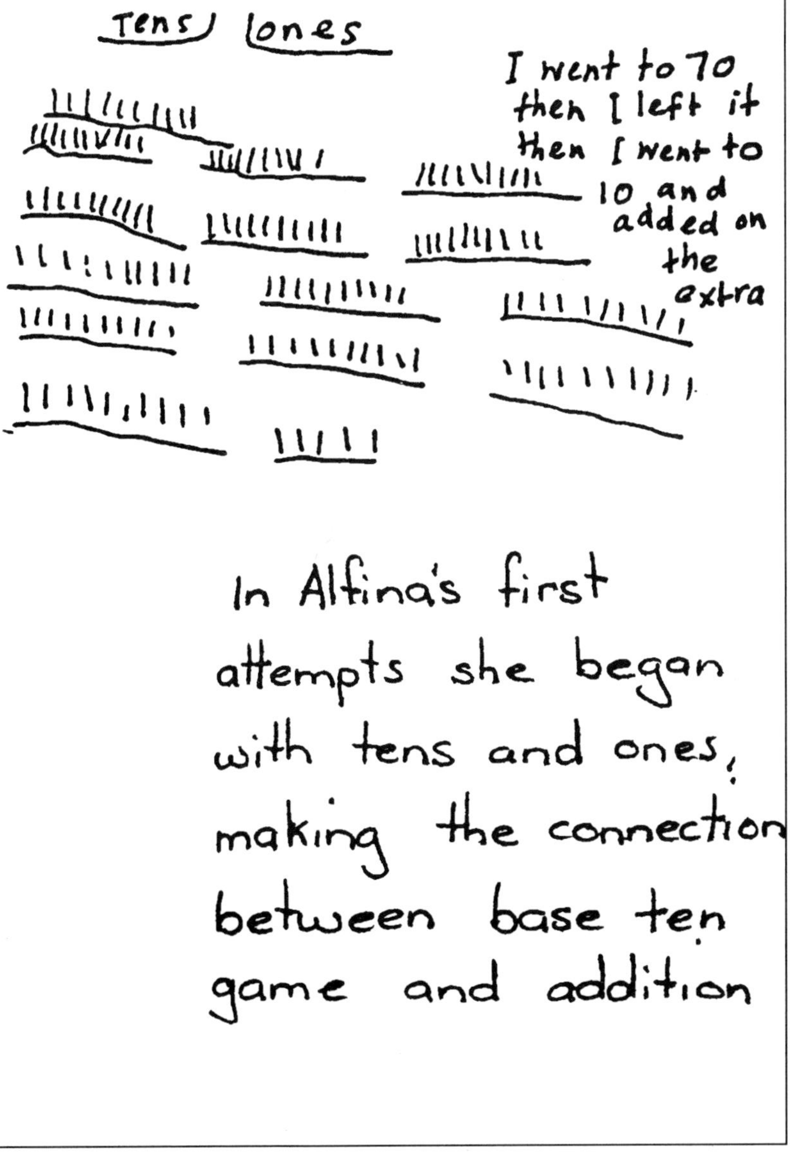

Tens / Ones

I went to 70 then I left it then I went to 10 and added on the extra

In Alfina's first attempts she began with tens and ones, making the connection between base ten game and addition

Figure 3.2

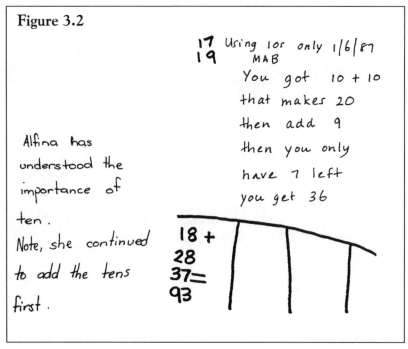

17
19

Using 10s only 1/6/87
MAB

You got 10 + 10
that makes 20
then add 9
then you only
have 7 left
you get 36

Alfina has
understood the
importance of
ten.
Note, she continued
to add the tens
first.

18 +
28
37 =
93

Figure 3.3

Adam needed
to see the
groups of ten

22

Figure 3.4

$1\,9$

$7\,9$

~~I took~~

$2\,7\,\cancel{6}\,\cancel{5}\,\cancel{4}\,\cancel{8}$

$1\,8$

$1\,4\,\cancel{2}\,3$

Adam was
later capable
of re-negotiating
the groups to
make tens.

I took one
out of the 7 and
added it to 9
then I took
another one out
of 7 and added
to the other
9 then I took
2 out of 7 and
added it to 8.

Figure 3.5

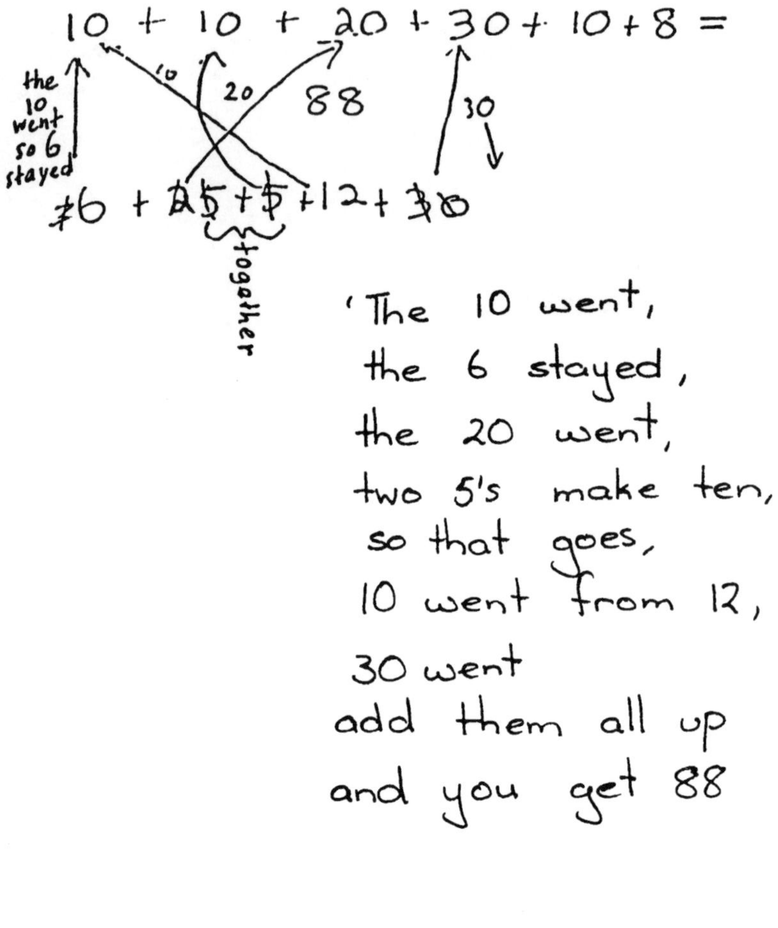

$$10 + 10 + 20 + 30 + 10 + 8 =$$

the 10 went so 6 stayed

10   20   88   30

$6 + 25 + 5 + 12 + 30$

together

'The 10 went,
the 6 stayed,
the 20 went,
two 5's make ten,
so that goes,
10 went from 12,
30 went
add them all up
and you get 88

Figure 3.6

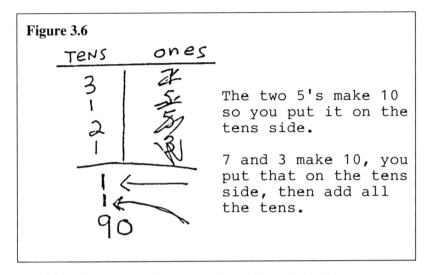

The two 5's make 10 so you put it on the tens side.

7 and 3 make 10, you put that on the tens side, then add all the tens.

Although unorthodox in method, the children's examples showed a high level of understanding. With many of their recordings I needed to write the child's explanation so that I would remember (see Figures 3.4 and 3.5). Never did I ask the children to write about what they had done. Recordings became not only the link between today's thinking and tomorrow's thinking for the children, but my own insight into each child's understanding.

Recordings, plus discussions equalled insight and understanding. I was no longer concerned about concrete activities being translated into abstract representations.

4
The teacher as learner

Base Ten proved to be a sound starting block. The children became confident in what they were doing and I gained valuable insight into my place in the mathematical classroom. I realised that:

- when children discover for themselves, they are more capable and willing to relate their knowledge to others
- children develop at different levels and I have to be sensitive to the individual and aware of when they are ready to be challenged further
- time is essential to any learning, and children must be given enough time to play, discuss, discover and share information
- my position is not one of teaching the children what I want them to know, but one of helping them to understand what they already know

- I must at no time underestimate what the children already know or what they are capable of doing.

Previously, the children had been working with Base Ten. I now needed to guide them from a concentration on number to a balanced curriculum including space and measurement. It was important to move slowly.

At the time, the school I was working in had developed its own school-based mathematics program. From this I listed the 'musts' for my class. For example:

- to add numbers up to 20
- to count forward to 100
- to count backward from 50
- to identify half
- to identify basic shapes and their attributes.

With a list like this, I felt I could try new ideas and methods within the boundaries of the curriculum. From a small group playing Base Ten, and now involved in addition and subtraction using dice and variations of Base Ten, we became a classroom of students working on different areas of number through Base Ten and the reintroduction of patterning and sorting.

How could I cover the areas of measurement and space? Again, using a list of what the children needed to know, I developed a problem book—a large newsprint scrapbook. A new problem was written into the book each day and included things like:

- How many different ways can you present 10?
- How many square-based pyramids can you make using polygons? Record the size of each base. Is there a pattern?
- How many different polygons can you make on the big geoboard? Can you record them?

The problems, fashioned to provide further challenge, were structured around the set curriculum and from work the children were doing. The children were free to work on the day's problem or to continue with the previous day's work. They could also go back to the problems of earlier days when they felt they were able.

I knew I was covering curriculum content, and I had provided myself with enough freedom to work within that structure. My confidence increased because of the safety of my list and I was learning to observe children and examine their recordings in order to find links in their thinking.

I then had to find ways of programming what I was doing. At no time had restrictions or prescriptions been placed on programming, either from Helen or from my principal. I was given the opportunity to develop a form of programming that suited me. Even now, when I am involved with teacher education, this is one of their first queries. I find myself continually explaining that programming is personal and, as long as it serves as a record of what the children are doing and how their thinking is developing, it has served its purpose.

I found that my former method of programming

was not suitable, nor could it be altered. My aims were now long-term and I no longer relied on what children appeared to achieve by the end of a lesson or a week of lessons.

My early programming efforts were retrospective. I had my list of what the children needed to know (my long-term objectives) and experimented with materials and activities that I felt would help them to work towards achieving the objectives.

Figure 4.1	
Week 1	patterning grouping of ten
Patterning	continued patterning introduce recording of patterns by: • pasting • drawing • writing about • photos • taping.
Grouping of ten	Grouping of popsticks into groups of ten with rubber bands around them.
Evaluation	Patterning has improved, however it is very interesting to note that the children who have very little trouble with normal maths are still having considerable difficulty with this type of activity.

Figure 4.1 was my first attempt at programming. Note the unwillingness to break from old, time restrictions. Only two activities were planned which were intended to help me stay in control of the situation. The rest would have been programmed retrospectively, after observing the interaction between the children, the materials and me.

Figure 4.2 shows more forward thinking in the area of materials by actually listing the new materials to be used. The evaluation was a more informed one. It stated what the children were actually doing with the materials, and my own understanding began to appear.

Figures 4.3 and 4.4 show my present format and it is one that I am content with. The areas of objectives, strategies and evaluation are all addressed, although instead of the standard form:

What do I want the children to know?
(objectives)

How will I help them to know?
(strategies, materials, questions)

How will I know what they know?
(observable indicators: things to look for that tell me the children are progressing)

Figure 4.2

1 Patterning:	painting/pasting patterns paper chains
2 Sorting:	coloured macaroni tops
3 MAB:	continuation
4 Adding:	Annette one die Corrine units only James two dice

Evaluation:	Very interesting revelation, both these children added tens first then whatever was left over, eg: $45 + 64 =$ $40 + 60 = 100$ then $100 + 5 = 105$ then $105 + 4 = 109$
Adding:	Alfina started at first using tens and units and drawing the sum, eg: $2\ /$ tens units ////////// / ///////// / then refined it by using MAB blocks
Patterns:	Writing numbers with patterns Peter /// a pattern of 6 Wilson 3 3 6 This is the start of multiplication Other children are using random numbers Dialogue is needed with these children
Base Ten:	Progressing well. All children have bundled and played with the dice Writing of score interesting. Most children use 0 for place value, eg: 101 becomes 100 1
Sorting:	More practice needed with a lot of discussion for verbal classification

31

Perhaps the following table might make more sense:

What do I want the children to know?	How will I help them to know?	How will I know that they know?
Broad objectives, within which all children can achieve	Framework of questions and activities and materials to assist the children to achieve	Sequential steps children have been observed going through to reach objectives

Observable indicators (what we can actually see the children do) have become valuable in record keeping and evaluation. They provide a basis for further questioning. The indicators are a tool with which the teacher can see the progress of each child. If, as in Figures 4.3 and 4.4, they are thought through and written in sequence, then it becomes easy to question children and guide them to the next step. This point can be illustrated using Figure 4.3. If children can explain how they have sorted a group of given objects (indicator 6) they can be asked to count the objects (indicator 7) then, once they are aware that the number can be used to describe a group of objects (indicators 8 and 9), number and counting become real and valuable tools to work with (objectives 2 and 3).

Figure 4.3

Mathematics—Term 1

Strand	What do I want the children to know?	How will I help them to know?	How will I know that they know?
	OBJECTIVES	STRATEGIES	INDICATORS
Number	The children will: 1 Sort and classify objects into groups 2 Count items 3 Number items 4 Make simple patterns	1 Commercial and non-commercial materials to sort 2 Limit number of objects given 3 Limit number in each group 4 Objects that can be sorted and re-sorted according to colour, size, shape, texture, direction, use etc 5 Materials used in sorting	1 Compare objects in each group ✓ *colour* 2 Find similarities ✓ *size* 3 Sort according to *direction* above ✓ *texture* 4 Re-sort using another criteria ✓ 5 Attempt to classify objects ✓ 6 Generalise about what/how they *well* have sorted ✓ *done* 7 Count objects in each group ✓ *James ✱* 8 Classify *Mary ✱* according to number 9 Use number as a criteria for sorting ✓ 10 Record sorting without using number ✓ 11 Record using *Not* number *yet* 12 Identify pattern in the environment ✓

In Figure 4.4, if the children show interest in the specific materials used to demonstrate fractions (indicator 1) and stay on a task for some considerable time (indicator 2) showing interest in how the pieces fit together (indicator 3), they would

Figure 4.4

NUMBER AND SPACE OBJECTIVES	STRATEGIES/ ACTIVITIES
Fractions 1 Discovering $\frac{1}{2}$ $\frac{1}{4}$ $\frac{1}{5}$ $\frac{1}{8}$ $\frac{1}{10}$ of numbers, related to times tables 2 Discovering equivalence 3 Adding and subtracting fractions with common denominators 4 Discovering properties of solid shapes	1 Free play 2 Equivalence: show relationship between pieces and whole shape 3 Give pieces names in relationship to one whole 4 Show equivalence of colours—record 5 Prove: eg $\frac{2}{5} = \frac{4}{10}$ 6 Choose a shape 7 Observe 8 Make from paper/multilinks 9 Give it a name 10 Make a pattern for others to copy

INDICATORS

1 Show interest in materials 2 Stay on task 3 Ability to put pieces together to make one 4 Record 5 Explain what has been done 6 Name parts in relation to one 7 Combinations for one 8 Use for colours/fractional terms 9 Record in fractional terms only 10 Add fractions to make one	11 Add two or more fractions to make a fraction 12 Find relationship between them 13 Find as many equivalent fractions as possible 14 Name the shape 15 Reproduce it on paper 16 List number for faces/corners 17 Ability to create a pattern 18 Use of graph paper for pattern

be asked to record (indicator 4). They would then be seen as working towards achieving objective one.

Although time consuming, the work that is required on indicators is well worth the additional effort. I now use my indicators column to write comments and children's names. This serves as a quick means of evaluation and record keeping. For instance, in Figure 4.3 it is easy to see that colour, size, direction and texture are the main characteristics the children use for sorting. Most of the class can generalise and verbalise about what they have done. James and Mary are having difficulty counting and thus recording, using number, has not yet appeared. These working notes then give me a basis for my next term's program.

Let me make it clear that this would not be my only means of evaluation. When I first began to change the mathematics in my classroom I found record keeping very time consuming. As in programming, no requirements were set out for me as to the amount or type of records I needed to keep. However, when I began to see the type of thinking that emerged from the children and the extent to which each individual worked and progressed, I realised that extensive records were needed if I was to keep informed. I also realised that my fellow workers were showing interest in what was happening in my classroom, so I needed to know exactly how each child was progressing to demonstrate to others, and justify to myself, the value of what was happening.

Looking back, I see similarities in the way I kept

records when I first began to change in language and the way I kept them when I first began to change in mathematics. I went back to a way that was familiar to me, and a way I knew I could cope with. Some methods were useful and I have kept them. Others have been discontinued.

Following is a list of methods I have used.

- Checklist of concepts
These gave me an idea of what each child may have only touched on, but they didn't serve as a means of measuring understanding or as an indication of the thinking process involved. They actually gave a false picture of what children knew.

- Target groups
This was a means by which I targeted a group of children each day to talk with and observe. Ideally every child had some individual attention each week. This method was unsuccessful because I would inevitably be interrupted by others wanting me to see what they had done. I also found that I was missing out on the achievements of so many, by spending my time with some who needed time to work alone with their ideas.

- Walking notebook
This is what I always kept in my hand as I walked around the room, jotting down what each child was doing. This method failed because I was trying to make notes for every child, every day, an impossible feat that caused much frustration. What I do now is to ask the children for their

maths folders and write on the back what I have observed. This does not happen every day with every child.

- Maths folders
  Mine are made from a doubled piece of cardboard. As mentioned previously, if I observed a child working, thinking or doing something of interest, I recorded it on their folder. Earlier I would take all the folders home every fortnight, look at what was inside, then make a comment. I still do this occasionally to give me some indication of the progress of the class as a whole, but I find it easier now to make notes as the child is working.

- Recording sheets

  See Figures 4.5 and 4.6 for examples.

  I have found this strategy useful when there are a number of parent helpers in the room. The recording sheet is filled out by me (as in Figure 4.5)

Figure 4.5	
Name: *Mary*	Date: *3-7-90*
Materials used	What the child did
What I wanted the child to achieve	
number as an attribute *ordering numbers* *recording*	Where to next?

Figure 4.6	
Name: *Mary*	Date: *3-7-90*
Materials used	What the child did
Bottle tops	• *sorted tops into size*
	• *placed tops side by side*
	• *counted each and labelled*
	• *ordered by size then by number*
What I wanted the child to achieve	• *recorded using grid paper but found she had to stick sheets together*
number as an attribute *ordering numbers* *recording*	Where to next?
	1 square can equal more than 1 top

and given to the parent. The parent then sits with the child and fills out 'materials used' and 'what the child did' (as in Figure 4.6). I then use this to see that Mary needs to realise that one square on a grid can equal more than one bottle top—this would be 'Where to next?'. It should be noted that parents need to be instructed on using these recording sheets so that they do not feel that the child must achieve all the objectives set down. They may be either too difficult or too easy to achieve, in which case observation is the key so that the child continues to work to their potential.

• Children's recordings

I find the most profitable way of keeping track of each child individually and of the class as a whole, is to learn to read children's recordings and keep copies of them. These recordings offer accurate insight into a child's thinking and learning process.

Figure 4.7

To illustrate this point, Figures 4.7 and 4.8 both show the work of two separate children using dice and the concept of addition. In Figure 4.7, the two dice were thrown and the answer recorded as one die with the number in the centre. In Figure 4.8, the dots were recorded and then the answer. This example shows the use of the equals sign, whereas Figure 4.7 does not. Both children, however, have indicated that they understand addition and equals. In Figure 4.9, dot cards (10 cards with 1 to 10 dots on them) were used again to illustrate addition. Here the children found it necessary to draw both cards and the answer in the centre. Again the understanding is clear, even though the conventions of addition are missing.

The children themselves keep all their work in maths folders, and I keep my own copies of significant work to assist in compiling meaningful profiles. While record keeping is essential, it must

Figure 4.8

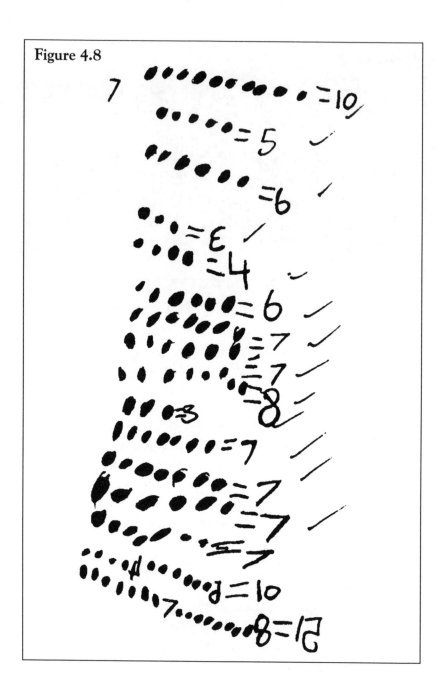

Figure 4.9

be remembered that mathematics is not the entire curriculum.

Record keeping is required in each subject area, so it must be kept simple and informative and as varied as the children and teachers themselves. What I realised is the importance of knowing where you are going (broad aims); of stepping back to observe what children are doing and of allowing them to express themselves and their thoughts.

5
The children

The following comments by the children showed an enthusiasm for maths that I had never experienced. The children wanted to share their mathematical achievements with their peers and other teachers.

I Like maths 'because you can do sortingpatterns graphs. Maths is my favorite thing in the class

Edward

I Like Maths Becouse it Good you Lurn Staf I$s herd it easy

And Amizing

I like maths
becaue its
fun and I
liorn thgs
and we
make gafs

I Like Maths because
it is fun and
Ecsetg and you lone

thengs

I Like maths because
it teaches you
Sart of how to think
hard and I like
to think hard and
you can chose what
you want to do by Natalie

> Maths is Fantastic
> BECAUSE
> you learn and you
> have fun. its
> hard Sometimes
> But it is still
> FUN.

Their reactions were not always favourable, however. The children also experienced their share of fears and frustrations. I recall the barrage of questions the first day I returned to my classroom with my new found knowledge of children and mathematics and proceeded to change all in one easy lesson.

'What's a pattern?'
'What do you mean?'
'How do you do it?'
'Is this right?'

Looking back, I realise that I had failed to take into account the security the children felt with the way maths had been presented to them in the past. They knew what was expected of them and they knew that if they paid attention to the demonstrations they would know 'how'. They also knew that if they didn't understand, I would sit with them and show them 'how'. Back then, after two days away, I had returned with vague requests and no indication that I was prepared to assist. They were lost. I don't know why I had thought they would be immune to the frustrations I was feeling. I had built my own framework for disaster.

These children had been achieving differing levels of success using standard methods. All of a sudden they had that familiar structure taken away. They needed guidance but, as I understood the philosophy of this 'new maths', the children were not to be given any instructions or answers. They would learn by osmosis.

Now, when working with my peers, I stress to them the importance of taking the time to understand why we put children into certain learning situations, what we expect them to achieve because of that situation, and how we can help them to achieve it. If these are not taken into account, only frustration and, in some cases, the rejection of a true learning method will occur.

I felt that the children's confidence stemmed from my own. Once I knew what to do and why I was doing it, I was more capable of altering my 'one question, one answer' technique to a form of open-ended questioning which required thinking, experimenting, discovery and proof.

For example:

- 'What number do you need to add to 4 to get the next squared number?'
- 'Is there a pattern in squared numbers?'
- 'Can you find the next squared number?'
- 'Can you see the pattern to find the 26th squared number?'

Once my attitude had changed and my knowledge had increased; once I allowed the children extended periods of time (one to one-and-

To Mrs murphy
I Love Beimng iN KM
AND I really DO
Love DOiNG mAths
I LoVe Schg L
FroM
CARLeen

a-half hours each day) to work with materials and develop ideas, we all became mathematics advocates with comments such as the one included from Carleen.

6
The parents

Embarking on a new way of teaching and learning, I felt it was important to invite parents to the classroom and tell them why the new direction had come about, what the children would be involved in and how they could become a part of that learning process.

Parent–teacher liaison needed to be frequent for parents to be kept informed and actively involved. I also believed it was important that the parents shared the excitement and enthusiasm that the children and I were experiencing.

I began by inviting the parents into the classroom so that they could experience the sense of achievement for themselves. The parents were briefed about not giving children the answers, and were always given time at the end of each visit to discuss what they had seen. It was the discussions that allowed them to gain insight into how the children thought.

After a couple of observation visits, many parents were eager to help on a regular basis, to either discuss with the children or to record the children's explanations of discoveries (see Figure 6.1).

Figure 6.1

Working in the classroom gives parents insight into children's thinking and makes them active partners in learning.

For those parents who were unable to visit the classroom, an anecdotal photo album was compiled showing the children at work. This album also became an excellent means of record keeping for me. Inside the cover of the album there was space for the parents to write comments. This served a twofold purpose. These comments indicated the parents' fears, frustrations and concerns. They also acted as a stimulus for those less interested. See Figure 6.2 for examples of some parents' comments

Figure 6.2.

First impressions, 'this is just not maths'. After many weeks of working with these very enthusiastic kids, for the first time in thirty years I'm actually enjoying maths. I often ask myself who is helping who. Both the kids and I have turned to being the instructor.

I have asked to re-enroll at school. What fun and what a mathematician I could have been if we'd been taught to enjoy maths. Having witnessed the sheer engrossing pleasure of these kids makes me envious.

Figure 6.2 *(cont)*

Brendan really enjoys doing maths and after seeing what the kids are learning, it is a more practical and enjoyable experience for them. This way of learning makes kids want to learn more and explore different ways of doing things on their own.

My first impression after watching KM doing maths in this way was, 'will they really learn something?', as they only appear to be playing, that was Term 1. Now we are closer to the end of the year and seeing how much each child has progressed I can only say thankyou Mrs Murphy and Mary Immaculate for making maths easy and enjoyable. (Yes, they really have learnt something.)

Figure 6.2 (*cont*)

From looking at this book and having seen the children in 1F doing maths this new way, I feel this method of teaching will be successful. My son in 1F seems to understand what he is doing, so I think I'm the one that will also have to learn this new method. Maybe then I will understand it better. I have yet to see 3B at work to see how they cope doing it this way. I suppose like every new way it takes time to adjust to different methods.

Parents needed to be comfortable with the program, so workshops were organised to provide them with more information about the mathematics being taught. Discussion was an integral part of each workshop, to help voice and answer any parental concerns (see Figure 6.3).

Figure 6.3

Old fears about mathematics are relived when parents are asked to participate in a task.

The parents were involved with some of the materials their children were using in the classroom. This helped to familiarise them with the names of various kinds of equipment and, most importantly, the types of question that might be asked by their children. Each parent workshop concentrated on a particular area of maths. For example: patterning, sorting, Base Ten or linear measurement.

Changes occurred in me, in my children and in their parents. All we needed was a chance to talk. It was not until I gave parents the time I was given, that I realised that growth had occurred in them. The following are some thoughts from parents.

When I first walked into my daughter's classroom, I
sensed total confusion. There were children in groups of
two, three or four all over the room playing with all sorts
of materials from blocks and popsticks to corks and lids
and twigs. It was clear that the children were having a
good time, but I felt that there was little learning going
on. I knew I had been invited to see learning, but I
wondered how there could be learning in all of this. Still
I decided to make the most of it, so I sat down to listen
to what the children were saying. It was in the listening
that I began to see beyond the play. These groups of
children were learning. As I moved around, I realised
that the children were all working at different levels and
all were comfortable in what they were doing. They were
all quite eager to tell me about it. It wasn't the way I
learnt, yet it was evident these children knew what they
were doing. I just needed time. What I did have was
trust in the teacher. She was always inviting the parents
in and sending photos home of what the children were
doing. Although I didn't have much time to visit, I still
felt like I belonged to the learning my daughter was
engaged in.

At home my daughter was and is always asking
questions about mathematics and I believe that if
children are asking questions then you can tell they are
learning.

Now, three years on, I feel that my daughter and I will
adapt to any mathematical learning situation. I believe she
has had the opportunity to develop lateral thinking that will
aid her not only in mathematics, but in life.

Charlie Monti

I was shocked at what I was invited into—a classroom of bedlam. I had expected it to be different to what I knew as a child, but this was a parent's nightmare. Children were playing everything with anything they could get their hands on. However, I was determined to see learning or to get my son out of there. The teacher was always inviting parents in and telling us to listen to what the children were saying about what they were doing: try not to tell them how to derive an answer—but that was very hard to do, especially when the answer was so close.

But I persisted. I listened to the children more than I spoke to them and it was them who taught me mathematics. My structured background made me feel so inadequate and here were these children who were being given the opportunity to discover and work out for themselves. I sensed the importance of the materials my son used. Whatever he could get his hands on at home to 'do maths'—he loved it and finally, after thirty years, I began to understand some of the 'whys' myself.

My son is now in a more traditional situation. He has had no trouble coping—in fact, he will often make the connection between what he is doing in class now to ways he was allowed to work things out then.

Julie Knox

I often look back on these comments when I feel frustrated or intimidated with the lack of understanding I encounter from some parents, and I realise that change is growth and both take time.

7
What makes a good start

I feel that I have indeed been fortunate. My progress can be attributed to the support of my principal and the interest and support of my peers, together with the availability of time to experiment and discuss. These are important factors for a good start but, in order to achieve effective and worthwhile change, there are other long-term factors to consider.

Principals who are supportive of change need to:

- perceive the need for change in the way mathematics is taught
- visit classrooms, attend in-services, talk to children in an attempt to make themselves familiar with current practice and up-to-date with the progress of the children

- make time available for discussing mathematics with all staff members during staff meetings and staff development days, so that all teachers are involved in some way with the change
- make time available for all staff members to visit one another and other schools involved in the same program, to allow for the sharing of ideas and resources and to set up inter-school support links
- be supportive of staff members during their frustrations by not imposing prescriptions and restrictions on their time, programming and record keeping
- make parents aware of change through parent nights and newsletters
- make money available for the purchase of materials.

The above can be summed-up by saying that maths should be made, for the moment, the number one priority in the school. This ensures that genuine efforts are put in at all levels. However, at no time should any person be asked to accept philosophies that they have not had the time or the opportunity to study, discuss, challenge and adjust for themselves.

It took me five months to realise that I needed to change the way in which I taught mathematics, and five years to work on the changes. This would not have been possible without the support of my peers and school hierarchy who provided encouragement, and more importantly, the time for change. I place my belief in the success of this change on what I have seen the children accomplish. I am convinced that both my work and that of the children is of high quality.

8
Evidence of change

If I had been asked four years ago 'What is change?' I would probably have said that change is the physical evidence of difference. Attitudes, feelings and beliefs may never have entered into it. Changing was doing something that was different.

Under close scrutiny, I see that some of the change that I undertook in regard to language was only cosmetic. I changed how I presented the lesson and how I dressed it up, but gave little or no thought about the attitudes I wished to nurture, the feelings I wished to influence or the beliefs I wished to inspire. Today when I think of change, it encompasses all of the above.

I had a negative attitude towards mathematics, fed by years of poor performance as a student and years of more basics as a teacher. Reading about mathematics or even looking beyond my class's requirements would have been unthinkable.

I now enjoy mathematics. I find it challenging. I work with other maths classes and assist with teacher education. I am not, in my opinion, mathematical, but I am willing to learn and ready to admit when I can't go any further. I can ask for help. This is the attitude I strive to foster in the children in my care.

Within the physical structure of the classroom there is also the evidence of change. For example:

- The classroom environment was:
  very much a language-centred classroom, because language was the area I personally felt comfortable with. I had (and still have) numerous books, graffiti board, children's own writing, signs, points of interest, so as to immerse children in print and instil in them the importance of reading and writing.

- Mathematics was locked away in books so that I could control it and call it out, only when I was ready to deal with those parts I felt comfortable with.

- The classroom environment is:
  mathematically stimulating. Materials are important: they are labelled and displayed.

  Children's work is displayed and used for discussion. Maths is evident when walking into the classroom.

- Materials were:
  used to demonstrate, rather than discover and explore. They had a similar purpose—different

materials for different concepts. Children needed to move away from using materials to using pen and paper as quickly as possible to prove that they had understood a particular concept. Materials needed to be commercially produced to be of any real value, because manufacturers knew better than I how to demonstrate a concept.

- Materials are:
  essential for the development of concepts and the clarification of ideas, so they are available for use at all times by children of all ages.

  Concrete materials allow children to move from concrete manipulation through pictorial representation and back again. By not specifying the use of each material, the children can choose which materials best help them.

  Junk materials (for example: bottle tops, corks, lengths of ribbon, timber off-cuts, shoelaces, perfume bottles), by their very nature, are non-specific in their use and, therefore, are invaluable in the maths classroom.

- Children's recordings were:
  ordered and conforming. They were mostly done in books.

- Children's recordings are:
  individual, both to the child and the teacher. Both the children and I feel comfortable with the means chosen. As previously mentioned, my children use paper which is then stored in maths folders. Other teachers I have worked with find it

easier to use scrapbooks for recordings. Whatever the means, it is how the recordings are used that is important.

- Record keeping was:
  based on checklists and weekly tests.

- Record keeping is:
  a means by which to map children's thinking.

My classroom is now a thinking classroom, where the children are in control of the learning within a clearly set framework.

I no longer fear mathematics as I once did. Because I have been challenged I can now challenge others. The most important change is in my belief in what I am doing. The process of change that I have worked through has influenced the core of my teaching. The children are the true centre of my classroom and their thinking is the guide to the structure of its environment.

The mathematician, Polya, once said:

'A great discovery solves a great problem, but there is a grain of discovery in the solution of any problem. The problem may be modest, but if it challenges your curiosity and brings into play your inventive faculties, and if you solve it by your own means, you may experience the tension and triumph of discovery. Such experiences at a susceptible age may create a taste for mental work and leave their imprint on mind and character for a lifetime.'